DIRECT OBSERVATION AND MEASUREMENT OF BEHAVIOR

Publication Number 763
AMERICAN LECTURE SERIES®

A Monograph in
The BANNERSTONE DIVISION *of*
AMERICAN LECTURES IN RADIATION THERAPY

Edited by
I. NEWTON KUGELMASS, M.D., Ph.D., Sc.D.
Consultant to the Departments of Health and Hospitals
New York City

Second Printing

DIRECT OBSERVATION AND MEASUREMENT OF BEHAVIOR

By

S. J. HUTT

Research Psychologist, Human Development Research Unit, Park Hospital for Children
Fellow of St. Catherine's College
Oxford, England

and

CORINNE HUTT

Research Psychologist, Human Development Research Unit, Park Hospital for Children
Research Fellow, Lady Margaret Hall
Oxford, England

CHARLES C THOMAS · PUBLISHER
Springfield · Illinois · U.S.A.

Published and Distributed Throughout the World by

CHARLES C THOMAS • PUBLISHER

Bannerstone House

301-327 East Lawrence Avenue, Springfield, Illinois, U.S.A.

© *1970 by* CHARLES C THOMAS • PUBLISHER

ISBN 0-398-00892-2

Library of Congress Catalog Card Number: 78-91850

First Printing, 1970
Second Printing, 1974

With THOMAS BOOKS *careful attention is given to all details of manufacturing and design. It is the Publisher's desire to present books that are satisfactory as to their physical qualities and artistic possibilities and appropriate for their particular use.* THOMAS BOOKS *will be true to those laws of quality that assure a good name and good will.*

Printed in the United States of America

N-1